Language Arts BINGO

10 Reproducible Bingo Games That Reinforce Skills in Grammar, Spelling, Vocabulary, and More

BY VIRGINIA MUSMANNO

SCHOLASTIC
PROFESSIONAL BOOKS

New York • Toronto • London • Auckland • Sydney • Mexico City
New Delhi • Hong Kong • Buenos Aires

Acknowledgements

*I would like to thank my family and friends for their encouragement as I published
my first book, with a special thanks to my daughter Lisa for her technical support, and reading
specialist Carrie Sowerby for consultations on lesson extensions. I also extend my gratitude
to my attorney Tom Wettach for his prudent advice and encouragement.*

*Diane Bell and her class at Sto-Rox Elementary Center
provided practice trials of the games; I appreciate their time and enthusiasm.*

*I also want to thank Kama Einhorn, my editor at Scholastic,
for her sensible advice in the design and format of this book.*

Cover design by **Maria Lilja**
Interior design by **Holly Grundon**

ISBN: 0-439-36545-7

Contents

Introduction

"BINGO!"

Most of us have had the pleasure of completing a row of plastic chips on a game card and triumphantly calling out that word. So why not bring the excitement of this fun and familiar game into the classroom, and use it to strengthen literacy skills?

Language Arts Bingo includes 10 Bingo games that provide fast-paced practice in key areas of your language arts curriculum. Students build word-recognition skills, develop their understanding of grammar concepts, and strengthen their spelling skills. They'll also build listening skills and learn teamwork. And all the while, they're having a good time!

GREAT FOR SECOND-LANGUAGE LEARNERS!

Students new to English can be very successful with the games in this book. The games will provide nonthreatening opportunities to learn words and grammar structures. Pair second-language learners with native English speakers. You might play the same game several times with these students, to reinforce the concepts introduced.

Using This Book

Each game is comprised of the following four pages:

TEACHER DIRECTIONS

Simple directions, tips, and extension activities help you and your students make the most of each game.

CALL LIST

This is a list of all the words the "caller" will call out during the game. (Cut along the dotted lines and put all the slips in an envelope before you begin to play.)

TEACHING Tip

Enlarge the cards if you wish. You might also laminate the cards for extra durability.

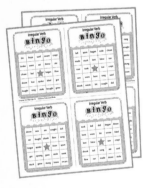

EIGHT STUDENT BINGO CARDS

Copy and cut apart the cards so that each student gets one. There are eight different cards, so several students will win at the same time. (Pair students together if you want to reduce the number of winning cards at one time.)

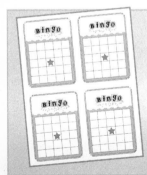

MAKE-YOUR-OWN GAMES

In addition, we've included four blank Bingo grids on page 7 so that students can make their own games on any topic!

◆ Students
  might enjoy
  being the
  caller as well.

◆ Give small
  prizes such
  as pretzels,
  animal
  crackers,
  stickers, or
  mini-erasers.

◆ Make up a
  sentence for
  each word
  called to
  put words
  in context
  and build
  vocabulary.

◆ Store the
  master call
  list, envelope
  with call-list
  words,
  Bingo cards,
  and chips
  in a large,
  self-sealing
  plastic bag.

Basic Instructions

These simple instructions apply to all 10 Bingo games.

1 Make two copies of the call list. Keep one copy intact, and cut apart the second one and place the slips in an envelope. (Making one of these on colored paper makes checking easier.)

2 Make copies of the bingo cards, cut them apart, and distribute so that each student or pair of students can have one. Distribute chips or markers.

3 Review the object of the game with students. Explain that a winner has five covered blocks in a straight line (vertically, horizontally, or diagonally).

4 Pull words from the call envelope and read them aloud. (As you go, place each slip on your master call list.) Students find the "answer" or corresponding word (depending on the game) on their card and add a chip or marker. Pause long enough between words to allow players to search their cards. Remind students to cover only one square for each word called.

5 When "Bingo" is declared, tell students to hold their cards. Say, "Clear your cards," once winners have been confirmed. Place the called words back in the envelope and, if desired, play again!

MARKERS

With a paper cutter, cut colored construction paper into small squares for chips. Keep the chips in sets of about 40 in individual envelopes or self-sealing bags. Students might also use the following as markers:

◆ Raisins

◆ Cinnamon red-hots

◆ Small buttons

◆ Candy-coated chocolates

◆ Dried beans

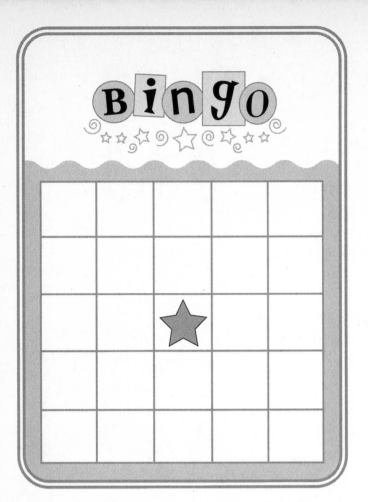

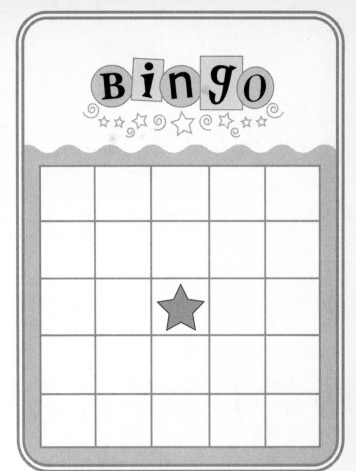

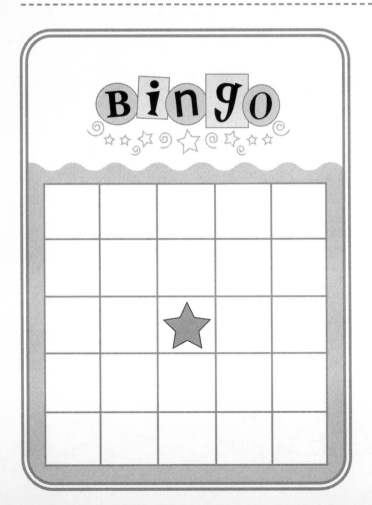

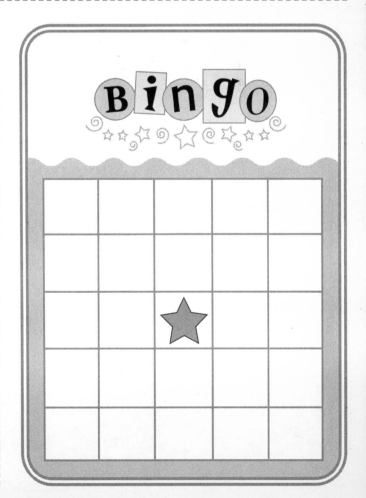

Advanced Word Family Bingo

The word families encountered in upper-grade reading are not always easily decodable or recognizable. Quick recognition of these spelling patterns is the focus of this game.

Advanced Word Family **Bingo**

ail	ain	air	awn	ead
eal	eat	eed	eight	ought
lef	oach	★	oil	ood
ook	ouch	ound	ow	ue
ew	aunt	eam		

PAGES 10–11

DIRECTIONS

1 Practice first by making copies of the call list (one per student). Have students circle or highlight the word-family "chunk" (ending sound) in each word. Taking turns, as a class or with partners, students should pronounce all words.

2 Play the game according to the Basic Instructions given on page 6: You say the word, and students place their markers on the corresponding word family on their card.

Try THIS!

TALK BACK

Pair students and pass out one Bingo card to each pair. Taking turns, one student reads a word chunk; the other provides a word with that chunk. Repeat for all chunks on the card. Reverse roles with another card. Or play the game with you as one player, and the class as the other.

BRAINSTORM

Write a word-family chunk on the board. In teams of three, have students write as many words as they can think of in that family. Set a time limit of a minute or two, then see which team has generated the most words.

SILLY SENTENCES

Ask pairs of students to write several silly rhyming sentences using words from the call list or from a particular word family. For example: *On a clear morning last year, I shook with fear because a big smear appeared on my ear!*

LIMERICKS

Word-family lists lend themselves nicely to limericks. Read a few limericks to familiarize the class with the format. Create a class limerick on the board using one of the word families. Or have pairs create their own limericks to read to the class!

TEACHING **Tips**

Send the call list home for extra spelling practice before playing the game.

To simplify the game, write the words on the board as you call them.

Call List   Advanced Word Family Bingo

bail	delight	complain	grief	unfair	brook	stream
assail	fright	explain	thief	deal	crook	crew
curtail	insight	obtain	good	heal	outlook	drew
frail	twilight	bread	hood	meal	undertook	mildew
trail	broil	dread	likelihood	steal	bellow	broom
brawn	coil	head	livelihood	zeal	burrow	bloat
drawn	foil	instead	understood	sleigh	shadow	caught
fawn	recoil	spread	bound	eighteen	glow	taught
lawn	spoil	agreed	found	weigh	void	appear
yawn	couch	bleed	ground	neighbor	gaunt	clear
bleat	crouch	deed	impound	freight	haunt	smear
cheat	grouch	feed	wound	broach	jaunt	boot
cleat	pouch	weed	affair	coach	beam	achieve
treat	slouch	belief	flair	bounce	give	believe
wheat	abstain	brief	impair	poach	gleam	grieve
blight	chain	chief	stair	roach	scream	float

Advanced Word Family

ail	ain	air	awn	ead
eal	eat	eed	eight	ought
ief	oach	⭐	oil	ood
ook	ouch	ound	ow	ue
ew	aunt	eam	ew	ief

Advanced Word Family

ounce	oot	oid	ieve	ear
aught	ue	oom	oat	ew
eam	aunt	⭐	ow	ook
oach	eigh	eal	rang	ound
ood	ief	eed	ue	awn

Advanced Word Family

ouch	ound	ow	ue	ounce
ight	ief	oach	oat	oid
ear	eam	⭐	eal	ead
awn	ail	aught	ow	oat
ail	eed	ight	eal	oil

Advanced Word Family

aught	eam	eight	ief	oil
aunt	eal	eed	ight	air
ead	eat	⭐	ail	ounce
oot	ue	oid	oom	ow
ound	ain	eigh	eal	eat

Advanced Word Family

eigh	eat	eam	ead	ief
ouch	ounce	ow	oid	eed
ail	air	★	aught	awn
eed	oach	ound	ue	ain
oid	air	eed	eal	oil

Advanced Word Family

ew	eed	ain	aunt	oom
ook	ead	ound	oid	ead
awn	aught	★	ail	ound
ood	ight	eat	awn	eigh
eed	ain	awn	oat	oot

Advanced Word Family

air	ight	ook	oat	eal
oach	ief	awn	oat	oid
ain	aught	★	ouch	oat
eat	air	aunt	ear	ieve
ouch	oil	eat	eed	ew

Advanced Word Family

ead	oid	ound	ail	aught
ook	ief	awn	ead	eat
ight	ound	★	oom	ounce
oil	awn	ail	oat	eat
ief	ead	eam	ieve	eigh

Contraction Bingo

Contractions make speech faster or less formal. To spell them correctly, students should understand that contractions are a way of combining two words, and that the apostrophe takes the place of missing letters.

Contraction BINGO

aren't	don't	I'll	I've	should've
couldn't	hadn't	I'm	let's	that's
could've	hasn't	★	she'll	they'll
didn't	haven't	it'll	she's	they're
doesn't	he's	it's		

PAGES 14–15

DIRECTIONS

1 Briefly review the concept of contractions. Correct placement of the apostrophe is often a problem; stress that it takes the place of the missing letters.

2 Play the game according to the Basic Instructions given on page 6. You read the two-word equivalent, students place their marker on its corresponding contraction.

TEACHING Tips

For spelling practice, ask each winner to spell the contractions in his or her "winning row."

Some students have trouble pronouncing contractions correctly. Have the winner pronounce all winning words.

SUNDAY PAPERS

Collect Sunday comics for several weeks and make black and white copies. Have students highlight the contractions in the comics. Tally them on copies of the call list. Compare tally sheets and analyze them to see if some contractions are more commonly used than others. Let students draw their own comic strip using at least one contraction in each frame.

CONTRACTION SKITS

Working in groups of three, students can write a short play on a theme of their choice. See which group can use the most contractions in their script. (They might use a copy of the call list for reference.)

CONTRACTION CONCENTRATION

Make a set of pronoun cards (you, we, she, I, and so on) and a set of cards with the contracted ending ('d, 're, 've, and so on). Lay all cards face down. Each player turns over two cards. If the player makes a contraction that can be read correctly, he or she keeps the cards. If not, he or she turns the cards back over in place. Players take turns until all cards are gone. The player with the most cards wins.

Call List   Contraction Bingo

are not	did not	had not
he is	is not	I have
she is	that is	they have
we are	will not	you will
could not	does not	has not
I will	it will	let us
should not	they will	was not
were not	would not	you are
could have	do not	have not
I am	it is	she will
should have	they are	we will
we have	would have	you have

Contraction Bingo

aren't	don't	I'll	I've	should've
couldn't	hadn't	I'm	let's	that's
could've	hasn't	★	she'll	they'll
didn't	haven't	it'll	she's	they're
doesn't	he's	it's	shouldn't	wasn't

Contraction Bingo

we'll	we're	weren't	won't	would've
you'll	you're	you've	isn't	aren't
could've	doesn't	★	haven't	I'll
it's	let's	she's	should've	they'll
they're	couldn't	didn't	don't	hasn't

Contraction Bingo

wouldn't	don't	it's	they're	you've
that's	won't	doesn't	it'll	they'll
should've	we've	★	didn't	isn't
I'll	shouldn't	weren't	could've	I'm
couldn't	we're	she's	he's	aren't

Contraction Bingo

hadn't	I've	they've	you'll	hasn't
let's	wasn't	you're	haven't	she'll
we'll	you've	★	aren't	I'll
that's	wouldn't	couldn't	I'm	he's
shouldn't	you'll	doesn't	she's	hadn't

Contraction Bingo

haven't	we'll	you're	let's	hadn't
they're	they've	it'll	wouldn't	isn't
won't	isn't	★	could've	should've
couldn't	shouldn't	aren't	she's	we're
doesn't	I'm	don't	they'll	I've

Contraction Bingo

haven't	hasn't	she'll	hadn't	let's
we'll	don't	I've	wasn't	you've
doesn't	it's	★	they've	you're
didn't	it'll	they're	you'll	could've
isn't	they'll	would've	couldn't	I'm

Contraction Bingo

didn't	I'm	won't	they'll	it's
hadn't	shouldn't	you'll	wasn't	she'll
he's	we're	★	couldn't	weren't
should've	aren't	isn't	doesn't	wouldn't
they're	I've	hasn't	you're	she'll

Contraction Bingo

you've	wouldn't	we're	they've	they'll
that's	you're	won't	we'll	they're
she'll	shouldn't	★	we've	wasn't
it's	let's	shouldn't	you'll	weren't
isn't	it'll	I've	she's	would've

Ending Blend & Digraph Bingo

The auditory discrimination of final consonant digraphs (two consonants that together make one sound) can be tricky. Most student practice concentrates on initial sounds rather than final consonant blends and digraphs. Here's a fun way to do just that!

Ending Blend & Digraph
Bingo

ch	nk	th	lt	ph
ld	nt	pt	mp	sh
lt	ph	★	nd	sk
mp	sh	ch	nk	th
nd	sk	ld		

PAGES 18–19

DIRECTIONS

1. Before playing, review all the letter pairs you will be using by writing each on the board and having the students pronounce them. Give or ask for an example word for each letter pair (for instance, *ch* is in *teach*).

2. Play the game according to the Basic Instructions given on page 6. You call the word; students put their markers on the corresponding digraph.

TEACHING
Tip

Remind students to cover only one square per word called.

IN THE NEWS
Bring in a newspaper and several highlighters. Have teams of students highlight as many ending consonant blends or digraphs as they can in a given amount of time.

Try THIS!

MATCHUP
Write the call-list words on index cards, leaving off the ending blend or digraph. Write the ending blends and digraphs on the board in a column. Pass out cards and have students attach self-sticking tape to the back as they receive their card. One at a time, have students stick their card next to an ending to make a real word.

DO-IT-YOURSELF DIGRAPHS
Using the blank Bingo grids on page 7, have students make their own Bingo card with new words, using the twelve ending blends and digraphs. They should list their words on a sheet of paper (without putting their name on it). Collect all papers, and play bingo by randomly calling out words from different students' lists.

Call List Ending Blend & Digraph Bingo

bench	adept	trunk	intelligent	shrimp
itch	slept	brash	print	skimp
match	wept	crash	serpent	autograph
peach	bald	polish	sprint	nymph
stitch	bold	rash	brisk	photograph
friend	emerald	relish	dusk	telegraph
intend	scald	asphalt	husk	triumph
mend	scold	cobalt	risk	booth
refund	blink	halt	whisk	fifth
offend	brink	salt	blimp	math
accept	bunk	tilt	limp	myth
adapt	shrink	absent	scrimp	north

Ending Blend & Digraph Bingo

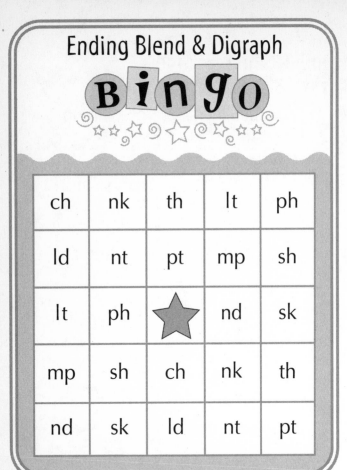

ch	nk	th	lt	ph
ld	nt	pt	mp	sh
lt	ph	★	nd	sk
mp	sh	ch	nk	th
nd	sk	ld	nt	pt

Ending Blend & Digraph Bingo

th	ph	nt	lt	nt
pt	sk	ld	nk	ld
sk	ch	★	ph	ch
sh	nd	ld	sh	th
mp	lt	nk	ch	ph

Ending Blend & Digraph Bingo

ch	lt	nd	nt	sh
th	ch	lt	nd	nk
ph	sk	★	pt	ld
mp	nt	sh	pt	lt
sk	nk	mp	th	ph

Ending Blend & Digraph Bingo

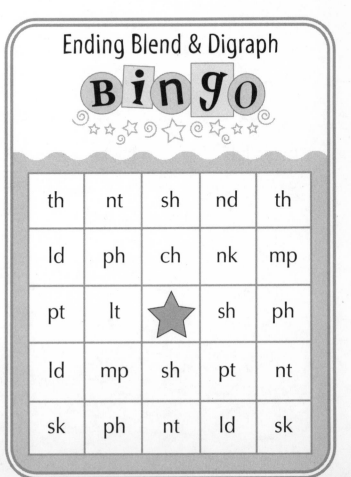

th	nt	sh	nd	th
ld	ph	ch	nk	mp
pt	lt	★	sh	ph
ld	mp	sh	pt	nt
sk	ph	nt	ld	sk

Ending Blend & Digraph

nd	nt	ld	mp	lt
ph	ld	nt	ch	lt
sh	ph	⭐	nd	ph
sk	nk	ch	sh	nk
pt	pt	th	sk	th

Ending Blend & Digraph

mp	nd	th	nd	ph
ph	sh	mp	nt	lt
nt	sh	⭐	sk	ph
nk	sk	lt	nk	th
ld	th	ld	ch	ch

Ending Blend & Digraph
Bingo

lt	nd	mp	sh	lt
ph	nk	ch	nd	nt
sk	ld	⭐	ld	mp
sk	th	ch	nk	th
nt	pt	mp	pt	sh

Ending Blend & Digraph
Bingo

pt	pt	nt	sh	nk
ph	mp	nd	ph	ch
lt	sk	⭐	ld	th
ld	mp	nt	nk	th
ch	nd	sh	sh	pt

Homophone Bingo

Homophones (words that sound the same but have different meanings) can cause confusion and spelling problems. Multiple exposures to the correctly spelled word can help!

Homophone
Bingo

aunt	due	inn	pale	sale
bee	feet	not	plane	waste
bored	great	★	write	bear
sell	hair	maid	sale	no
claws	hear	knight		

PAGES 22–23

DIRECTIONS

1 Copy the call list for the students. Discuss each pair of homophones and their meanings.

2 Play the game according to the Basic Instructions given on page 6. Pull one slip and read both words aloud. Use each in a sentence and discuss the different meanings. For instance, say *aunt, ant*. Pause. Say, *I love my Aunt Judy* (pause to have those with *aunt* on their card place their chip. Then ask for a volunteer to spell *aunt*.) Then say, *The ant ruined our picnic* (pause to have those with *ant* on their card place their chip). Ask for a volunteer to spell *ant*.

TEACHING
Tips

You might try some of the extension activities suggested below before playing this game, to lessen confusion.

Have the winners tell you not only the winning words, but also their meanings.

HOMOPHONE PAIRS

Ask each student to choose a pair of homophones to illustrate. Have them fold a piece of paper in half like a little book, then write a homophone on each side and illustrate each in turn.

Try THIS!

HOMOPHONE BEE

Have an old-fashioned spelling bee, dividing the class into two teams. Say a homophone pair. A student on one team spells the word and uses it correctly in a sentence; a member of the other team does the same for the homophone mate. (Alternate which team goes first, since the team who goes second will always have the more challenging task.)

AMELIA BEDELIA

Read an Amelia Bedelia story to the class. Have students write a short paragraph of their own Amelia Bedelia story. To get them started, ask, *What would Amelia do if you said, "Wash the hair on your head"*? (She would put a hare on your head and wash it!)

SENTENCE WRITING

Have students write logical sentences that include two homophones, such as:
- ◆ The students were bored with the math problems on the board.
- ◆ I asked the bookseller to look for an old book in his cellar.

Call List

Homophone Bingo

		hare	hair	scene	seen	dew	due
		pray	prey	cellar	seller	lessen	lesson
		blew	blue	in	inn	steal	steel
ant	aunt	haul	hall	see	sea	dye	die
flour	flower	right	write	cent	sent	made	maid
pail	pale	board	bored	knead	need	tail	tale
ate	eight	heal	heel	sew	so	fare	fair
grate	great	road	rode	clause	claws	mail	male
pause	paws	brake	break	knew	new	their	there
bare	bear	here	hear	soar	sore	feat	feet
groan	grown	rose	rows	creak	creek	meat	meet
peace	piece	by	buy	knot	not	waist	waste
be	bee	hole	whole	son	sun	flee	flea
guest	guessed	sail	sale	dear	deer	one	won
plain	plane	cell	sell	know	no	wood	would
been	bin	hour	our	stair	stare	night	knight

Homophone Bingo

aunt	due	inn	pale	sale
bee	feet	not	plane	waste
bored	great	⭐	write	bear
sell	hair	maid	sale	no
claws	hear	knight	sore	buy

Homophone Bingo

eight	here	by	rode	sun
bin	flea	hole	blew	waist
rose	cell	⭐	creek	be
scene	in	meet	soar	plain
sent	knew	be	grate	one

Homophone Bingo

flea	won	would	fare	bee
tale	deer	maid	sun	sent
not	see	⭐	buy	inn
rode	blue	hear	plane	bear
hair	pale	great	steel	hall

Homophone Bingo

rows	break	sea	cent	creak
heel	hear	doe	knead	knot
road	whole	⭐	so	son
sail	sell	seen	clause	meat
pail	hour	cellar	new	sore

Homophone Bingo

dough	mail	sell	here	see
by	pause	waste	write	their
hole	pray		bee	sun
fare	one	tail	piece	knight
meat	road	groan	aunt	fair

Homophone Bingo

rode	fair	sea	whole	right
ant	be	won	there	waist
made	know		meet	son
night	mail	ate	board	right
tale	fare	won	wood	grate

Homophone Bingo

dye	ant	our	guest	cellar
male	paws	need	flour	blew
lesson	do		be	pray
their	bare	peace	been	no
feat	grown	heal	brake	stair

Homophone Bingo

dough	pause	sew	do	flee
flower	hare	dear	lessen	waist
guessed	pray		steal	hear
plain	blue	board	die	feet
bin	haul	know	stare	there

Irregular Verb Bingo

Most past tense verbs are formed by adding *-ed*. However, students need to read and write irregular verbs, too!

Irregular Verb Bingo

bit	froze	said	swam	crept
broke	went	set	threw	ate
chose	led	★	began	flew
drove	lost	spoke	bled	got
fought	rang	stole		

PAGES 26–27

DIRECTIONS

1. To familiarize students with irregular verbs, copy the call list for each student and read each present-tense verb aloud. Invite the class to "echo" its past tense in response. Depending on students' levels, they can cover up the past tense column. Tell students to "think yesterday!"

2. Play the game according to the Basic Instructions given on page 6. Call out a present tense verb, and have students look for its past tense equivalent on their card. Ask for a volunteer to use the past tense verb in a sentence.

TEACHING Tip

As you call the verbs, use them in sentences to keep them in context.

Try THIS!

SWITCHEROO!
Have half the class write a sentence using a present tense verb (each student using a different verb). Ask the other half of the class to write sentences using past tense verbs. "Presents" switch with "pasts" and rewrite the sentence on the page in the opposite tense.

PAST-TENSE CHARADES
Pick past-tense verbs from the call list and have children act them out as the rest of the group guesses the word.

PAST-TENSE MEMORY
Start a story and go around the circle, with each student repeating all that was said previously. For instance:

Teacher: I went on a trip.

Student 1: I went on a trip. I brought a good book to read.

Student 2: I went on a trip. I brought a good book to read. I wore my new tennis shoes.

Call List
Irregular Verb Bingo

		fly	flew	say	said
		forget	forgot	see	saw
begin	began	freeze	froze	seek	sought
bend	bent	get	got	set	set
bite	bit	give	gave	shake	shook
bleed	bled	go	went	sing	sang
blow	blew	grow	grew	speak	spoke
break	broke	know	knew	spin	spun
bring	brought	lead	led	spring	sprang
catch	caught	leave	left	steal	stole
choose	chose	lend	lent	stick	stuck
creep	crept	lose	lost	sting	stung
do	did	make	made	swim	swam
drive	drove	ride	rode	take	took
eat	ate	ring	rang	throw	threw
fall	fell	rise	rose	wear	wore
fight	fought	run	ran	write	wrote

Irregular Verb

Bingo

bit	froze	said	swam	crept
broke	went	set	threw	ate
chose	led	★	began	flew
drove	lost	spoke	bled	got
fought	rang	stole	bought	grew

Irregular Verb

Bingo

left	spun	began	rode	chose
made	stuck	lent	blew	ran
rose	took	★	lost	crept
saw	wore	bent	rang	said
shook	wrote	bit	caught	did

Irregular Verb

Bingo

drove	saw	ate	sought	fell
set	fought	shook	flew	sang
forgot	spoke	★	froze	spun
got	sprang	gave	stole	went
stuck	grew	stung	knew	swam

Irregular Verb

Bingo

took	led	did	began	threw
bent	wore	bit	wrote	bled
lent	blew	★	saw	crept
shook	fell	sang	ate	said
flew	ran	made	drove	stole

Irregular Verb

began	bent	bit	bled	blew
broke	brought	caught	chose	crept
did	drove	⭐	fell	fought
flew	forgot	froze	got	gave
went	grew	knew	led	left

Irregular Verb

lent	lost	made	rode	rang
rose	ran	said	saw	sought
set	shook	⭐	sang	spoke
spun	sprang	stole	stuck	stung
swam	took	knew	threw	wore

Irregular Verb

wrote	crept	gave	made	sang
bent	drove	grew	rang	spun
bled	fell	⭐	ran	stole
broke	flew	led	saw	stung
caught	froze	lent	set	took

Irregular Verb

Bingo

threw	wrote	began	bit	blew
brought	chose	did	ate	fought
forgot	got	⭐	went	knew
left	lost	rode	rose	said
sought	shook	spoke	sprang	stuck

Prefix Bingo

Morphemic analysis is one of the most important skills needed for proficient reading in the intermediate grades. Quick recognition of prefixes builds students' fluency and comprehension.

DIRECTIONS

1 Play the game according to the Basic Instructions given on page 6 (but make several copies of the call list and cut apart since you'll use each prefix multiple times). You call out the prefix (and copy it onto the board), and students find a word containing that prefix on their card.

2 As you introduce each prefix, have students call out the words they've placed markers on. Write those words on the board under the prefix. Discuss the meaning of each word, or challenge students to use each one in a sentence.

PAGES 30–31

TEACHING

Tips

If your students' knowledge of prefixes is limited, try some of the extension activities given below first.

Remind students to cover only one word for each prefix called.

DICTIONARY SEARCH

In a given time period, have pairs of students use a dictionary to find one, two, or more words with the same prefix.

PREFIX CONCENTRATION

Write the different prefixes on index cards, and words that will complete the word on another set of index cards (for instance, "un" on one card, "fair" on the other.) Turn the cards over and play Concentration.

PIN THE TAIL ON THE PREFIX

Draw a simple donkey shape (or have a student volunteer draw one), and write all the prefixes from the call list in the donkey. Blindfold a student and have him or her attach a paper tail to the donkey. Take off the blindfold and look at the prefix closest to the point on which the student "pinned the tail." The student then writes a word with that prefix on the board.

Call List   Prefix Bingo

ad- (toward, before)	post- (after)
dis- (from)	pro- (for)
im- (not)	tri- (three)
out- (from)	de- (from)
ir- (not)	in- (not)
super- (above)	mis- (bad)
bi- (two)	pre- (before)
ex- (from)	sub- (under)
inter- (between)	un- (not)

Prefix Bingo

ad-dress	pre-pare	ex-aggerate	bi-focals	pre-view
inter-fere	de-part	im-perfect	inter-section	de-value
out-doors	in-direct	★	ad-mire	in-sincere
post-pone	bi-annual	ex-cite	im-polite	dis-turb
post-script	dis-agree	mis-cast	out-law	mis-chief

Prefix Bingo

ir-regular	ad-mire	ir-relevant	de-part	ir-responsible
super-fine	ex-ample	super-impose	pro-fessor	pro-file
pro-duce	un-afraid	★	tri-color	in-direct
tri-angle	dis-turb	sub-merge	out-burst	sub-mit
sub-side	un-lit	pre-historic	post-pone	sub-due

Prefix Bingo

in-complete	un-lit	pre-pare	mis-cast	out-dated
sub-marine	post-date	in-tern	un-fed	ir-regular
ir-responsible	sub-due	★	mis-behave	super-fine
un-afraid	out-doors	ex-am	pro-found	post-man
ex-cept	dis-agree	pre-dict	super-human	un-spent

Prefix Bingo

in-sincere	sub-due	bi-monthly	dis-array	pre-view
de-part	ex-aggerate	ad-here	ir-regular	im-mortal
in-complete	pre-pare	★	in-ablilty	dis-agree
mis-cast	bi-annual	de-canter	out-doors	ad-just
inter-fere	in-visible	sub-merge	sub-side	inter-pret

Prefix Bingo

bi-annual	super-fine	out-burst	un-afraid	ex-aggerate
ad-dress	in-ability	bi-ceps	de-caffinate	post-date
tri-angle	pre-dict	⭐	ad-dict	ir-rational
dis-ability	de-canter	im-mortal	dis-agree	inter-cept
ex-am	mis-behave	pro-claim	in-complete	sub-due

Prefix Bingo

im-patient	out-dated	post-man	ex-ample	in-direct
pre-historic	ad-here	sub-marine	pro-duce	out-doors
mis-cast	dis-appoint	⭐	bi-cycle	post-nasal
un-fed	ir-regular	im-perfect	inter-fere	in-tern
de-ceased	mis-chief	super-human	Tri-ceratops	pre-judice

Prefix Bingo

ir-relevant	super-impose	ad-just	de-part	im-possible
ex-cept	out-field	inter-pret	pro-fessor	dis-array
ir-responsible	tri-color	⭐	un-just	sub-merge
mis-conduct	pre-pare	in-sincere	bi-focals	post-pone
super-man	sub-mit	tri-cycle	pro-file	un-lit

Prefix Bingo

ex-cite	de-value	super-natural	in-visible	tri-ple
im-polite	out-law	inter-section	dis-turb	bi-monthly
pre-view	ir-responsible	⭐	ad-mire	tri-angle
un-spent	mis-fit	un-just	sub-side	ad-dict
pro-found	super-impose	post-script	bi-ceps	out-field

Suffix Bingo

Grammatically, suffixes are somewhat more difficult than prefixes. The suffixes *-age*, *-ary*, *-ment*, *-ness*, *-ship*, and *-tion* often indicate nouns. Words with *-able*, *-ful*, *-ial*, *-ible*, *-ic*, and *-less* are usually adjectives. Endings such as *-ate*, *-ify*, and *-ize* often indicate verbs.

Suffix Bingo

fal-sify	organ-ize	form-less	encamp-ment	sleepi-ness
disas-trous	horse-man-ship	two-some	celebra-tion	avail-able
extens-ive	ceme-tery	★	oper-ate	fin-ery
joy-ful	so-cial	flex-ible	hero-ic	clas-sify
empha-size	friend-less	entertain-ment		

PAGES 34–35

DIRECTIONS

1 Play according to the Basic Instructions given on page 6 (but make several copies of the call list since you'll use each suffix multiple times). You call out the suffix (and copy it onto the board), and students find a word featuring that suffix on their card.

2 After each suffix is introduced, have students call out the words they've placed markers on. Write those words on the board under the suffix. Discuss the meaning of each word, and challenge students to use each one in a sentence.

3 Have the winner name the part of speech to which each of his or her winning words belongs

TEACHING

Tips

Remind students to cover only one word for each suffix called.

Copy the call list onto a transparency and tally on the overhead projector.

Try THIS!

BINGO BRAINSTORM

On the board, brainstorm other words with these suffixes that could have been included but were not. Generate at least 24. (A rhyming dictionary might be of help.) Using the blank Bingo grids on page 7, let each student randomly write the brainstormed words in any order on his or her card. Play Bingo with the newly generated words.

SUFFIX LONG JUMP

Divide the class into two teams. Pull a suffix out of the call envelope. The first team member must think of a word that ends with that suffix in 10 seconds. If he or she succeeds, he or she jumps from the starting line, and remains there while the other team's first member gets a chance. Return the suffixes to the envelope after each turn. The next member of the first team then has to jump from the first member's spot if he or she provides a word with the next newly drawn suffix. Play continues until all members have a chance to call out a word. The winning team is the one farthest from the starting line.

Call List   Synonym & Antonym Bingo

SYNONYM GAME	WORDS ON CARDS	ANTONYM GAME
start	begin	stop
immature	childish	mature
chilly	cool	warm
postpone	delay	accelerate
rapid	fast	slow
scared	fearful	brave
unwise	foolish	smart
pal	friend	enemy
ample	full	empty
glad	happy	downcast
firm	hard	soft
torrid	hot	cold
enormous	huge	tiny
sick	ill	healthy
allow	let	forbid
noisy	loud	quiet
attractive	lovely	hideous
fortunate	lucky	unfortunate
important	necessary	unimportant
flawless	perfect	imperfect
close	shut	open
immerse	sink	rise
grin	smile	frown
cheap	stingy	generous
powerful	strong	weak
sugary	sweet	sour
exhausted	tired	rested
incomplete	unfinished	done
disappointed	unhappy	delighted
feeble	weak	strong

Synonym & Antonym

let	hot	fearful	tired	hard
full	stingy	ill	fast	perfect
lovely	shut	⭐	strong	loud
foolish	cool	unhappy	friend	delay
sweet	begin	huge	weak	sink

Synonym & Antonym

lucky	fast	huge	full	let
happy	weak	ill	lovely	shut
smile	stingy	⭐	cool	perfect
sink	hot	begin	fearful	necessary
childish	foolish	sweet	begin	unfinished

Synonym & Antonym

unhappy	friend	loud	delay	unfinished
huge	foolish	sweet	hot	necessary
tired	strong	⭐	begin	childish
hard	fast	ill	fearful	sink
weak	perfect	lucky	happy	smile

Synonym & Antonym

lovely	cool	tired	perfect	smile
necessary	loud	fast	begin	foolish
let	stingy	⭐	unhappy	weak
lucky	sink	unfinished	friend	ill
hot	full	shut	huge	hard

Synonym & Antonym

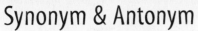

let	full	lovely	stingy	shut
cool	unhappy	huge	tired	weak
hard	perfect	★	lucky	happy
smile	sink	childish	necessary	unfinished
delay	loud	friend	strong	fast

Synonym & Antonym

ill	fearful	begin	hot	sweet
foolish	let	lovely	stingy	shut
cool	unhappy	★	huge	tired
weak	hard	perfect	lucky	happy
smile	sink	childish	loud	friend

Synonym & Antonym

full	perfect	friend	foolish	tired
stingy	happy	fast	let	hard
cool	sink	★	lovely	lucky
huge	necessary	fearful	shut	smile
weak	delay	hot	unhappy	childish

Synonym & Antonym

unfinished	begin	full	sink	necessary
huge	loud	sweet	stingy	delay
friend	weak	★	fearful	cool
foolish	fast	perfect	strong	hot
let	lovely	shut	happy	ill

Parts of Speech Bingo

In this game, students will build their awareness of different parts of speech—and begin to identify them more rapidly.

DIRECTIONS

1 So that everyone is familiar with the names of the different parts of speech, play a sample game first where you all decide together which part of speech was called.

2 Play according to the Basic Instructions given on page 6. You say the word, and students place a marker on one square that indicates which part of speech the word is.

PAGES 42–43

TEACHING Tip

You may have multiple winners as often as every four calls, unless you play double Bingo (having Bingo two different ways) or have winners fill every square on the card.

Try THIS!

DEFINE YOUR TERMS

You might define the different parts of speech like this:

A *noun* names a person, a place, or a thing.

Proper nouns name specific people or places, and are capitalized.

A *pronoun* takes the place of a noun.

Verbs are words describing the action that's taking place.

Adjectives are words that describe nouns.

Adverbs tell how, when, where, or how much.

An *article* comes before a noun: *a, an,* or *the.*

Prepositions show the relationship between a word and its object.

MAKE YOUR OWN MAD LIBS

Brainstorm a list of words for one part of speech. Have students read a paragraph in any book and identify all the words that are that part of speech, then substitute those words for the words brainstormed. They can read the silly new paragraphs to the class.

CONTENT-AREA BINGO

Instead of using the call cards, call out vocabulary words from your social studies, science, or language arts curriculum.

Call List — Parts of Speech Bingo

a	library	we	grow	cute	costly	at
an	moth	they	hear	famous	easily	before
the	mother	you	know	happy	joyfully	during
America	movie	they	knock	hot	later	fo
Vermont	president	them	leave	large	now	rrom
Abraham	restaurant	I	like	long	once	in
Lincoln	side	me	listen	old	dly	into
Joseph	sister	us	passed	popular	quickly	of
Mrs. Smith	sofa	him	read		quietly	off
Dr. Potter	sport	accept	sing	short	slowly	on
New York	teacher	admit	s	silly	twice	over
bird	tree	appear	teach	small	above	under
boy	he	bro	typed	sweet	after	up
fog	her	do	awful	tall	against	with
gym	she	forget	beautiful	constantly	along	without
kitchen		gave	black	correctly	around	loudly

Parts of Speech

Bingo

verb	preposition	noun	proper noun	pronoun
adjective	article	adverb	verb	preposition
noun	proper noun	★	pronoun	adjective
article	adverb	verb	prep-osition	noun
proper noun	pronoun	adjective	article	adverb

Parts of Speech

Bingo

pronoun	adjective	article	adverb	verb
preposition	noun	proper noun	pronoun	adjective
article	adverb	★	verb	preposition
noun	proper noun	pronoun	adjective	article
adverb	verb	preposition	noun	proper noun

Parts of Speech

Bingo

adverb	verb	preposition	noun	proper noun
verb	preposition	noun	proper noun	pronoun
adjective	article	★	adverb	verb
preposition	pronoun	adjective	article	adverb
noun	proper noun	pronoun	adjective	article

Parts of Speech

Bingo

pronoun	adjective	article	adverb	verb
preposition	noun	proper noun	pronoun	noun
proper noun	pronoun	★	adjective	article
adverb	verb	preposition	noun	proper noun
adjective	article	adverb	verb	preposition

Parts of Speech

noun	proper noun	pronoun	adjective	article
adverb	verb	preposition	noun	proper noun
pronoun	adjective	★	article	adverb
verb	preposition	noun	proper noun	pronoun
adjective	article	adverb	verb	preposition

Parts of Speech

article	adverb	verb	preposition	noun
proper noun	pronoun	adjective	article	adverb
verb	prep-osition	★	noun	proper noun
article	adverb	verb	preposition	pronoun
adjective	article	adverb	noun	proper noun

Parts of Speech

preposition	noun	proper noun	pronoun	adjective
article	adverb	verb	preposition	noun
proper noun	pronoun	★	adjective	article
adverb	verb	preposition	preposition	noun
proper noun	pronoun	adjective	article	verb

Parts of Speech

verb	preposition	noun	proper noun	pronoun
adjective	article	adverb	verb	preposition
noun	proper noun	★	pronoun	adjective
article	adverb	verb	preposition	noun
proper noun	pronoun	adjective	article	adverb

Syllable Bingo

If students can hear the number of syllables in words, they can decode multi-syllabic words more easily, which helps them become more fluent readers and better spellers.

DIRECTIONS

1 Play the game according to the Basic Instructions given on page 6. When pronouncing the word from the call list, say it three times for clarity:

- ◆ Slowly, enunciating each syllable

- ◆ At a normal rate of speed, the way it is naturally pronounced

- ◆ Slowly again, enunciating each syllable

2 Students place a marker on the numeral that corresponds to the number of syllables in the word you've pronounced.

TEACHING Tips

Remind students to cover only one square for each word called.

The game will produce many winners quickly. Playing "fill the card" will lengthen the game.

Have students clap out the syllables they hear in a word.

PAGES 46–47

SYLLABLE STROLL

Try THIS!

Cut index cards in half (puzzle piece-style, so that no two cards fit together the same way—this will serve as a self-checking device). Put the first part of a two-syllable word on one half, the other part on the second half. Shuffle the cards and give one to each student. Let students walk around the room until they find a partner who makes a match for a real word. After all partners are matched, have the students read their words to the class. This game can also be played with three-, four-, and five-syllable words (use larger cards or sentence strips).

SYLLABIC SENTENCES

Have pairs of students create one sentence with as many one-syllable words as possible. Then have them try it with as many two-, three-, four-, and five-syllable words as possible in one sentence. Or have them try their hand at writing haiku (first line, five syllables; second line, seven; third line, five).

Call List
Syllable Bingo

		loyal	presented	superhuman
		napkin	recapture	temperature
		science	triangle	transportation
dirt	thirst	skillful	unfairness	conversational
annoy	strike	station	automobile	educational
flow	thought	carnival	activities	inaccurately
flute	true	determine	biography	inarticulate
king	ashore	drowsiness	disappointed	inconsiderate
kite	candle	enormous	disapproval	interdependent
kneel	circus	expensive	generation	irresistible
news	dainty	gorilla	impossible	irresponsible
queen	daughter	impatient	inflexible	manufacturing
quiz	dislike	magazine	nonproductive	precipitation
quote	double	midsummer	responsible	unintentional
rest	laundry	October	rhinoceros	unprecedented
soup	lawful	passenger	subtropical	unprofessional

Syllable Bingo

1	5	1	5	5
2	4	2	1	1
3	3	★	2	2
4	2	3	3	3
5	1	4	4	4

Syllable Bingo

1	1	1	2	2
2	2	3	3	4
4	4	★	1	2
3	4	5	1	2
3	4	5	1	2

Syllable Bingo

4	4	4	5	5
2	3	3	3	4
2	1	★	1	4
3	2	2	2	5
3	1	1	4	1

Syllable Bingo

1	2	3	4	1
2	3	4	5	2
3	4	★	2	4
2	5	4	5	2
4	2	1	4	1

Syllable Bingo

2	4	1	1	1
5	5	2	4	3
1	5	★	5	3
2	4	1	2	4
1	2	4	3	3

Syllable Bingo

1	5	4	2	4
1	2	1	5	3
5	2	★	2	1
3	1	3	3	3
5	4	2	4	4

Syllable Bingo

1	2	3	4	5
1	2	3	4	5
3	3	★	2	2
4	4	5	5	1
1	1	3	5	2

Syllable Bingo

3	5	3	5	2
4	1	4	1	3
2	5	★	2	5
1	2	1	2	3
3	3	4	4	4

Call List   Suffix Bingo

-able (can be)	-ize (to make)
-ate (to have or be characterized by)	-ness (a state of being)
-ial (relating to)	-some (having the quality of)
-ify (make or become)	-ary (a place of)
-ment (a state of being)	-ful (full of)
-ship (condition of being)	-ic (relating to)
-ive (doing some action)	-less (lack of)
-ery (a place of)	-ous (full of)
-ible (can be)	-tion (a state of being)

Suffix Bingo

fals-ify	organ-ize	form-less	encamp-ment	sleepi-ness
disastr-ous	horse-man-ship	two-some	celebra-tion	avail-able
extens-ive	cemet-ery	★	oper-ate	fin-ery
joy-ful	soc-ial	flex-ible	hero-ic	classi-fy
emphas-ize	friend-less	entertain-ment	happi-ness	nerv-ous

Suffix Bingo

friend-ship	hand-some	informa-tion	regrett-able	prob-able
extens-ive	select-ive	avi-ary	cemet-ery	celebr-ate
illus-trate	bak-ery	★	fin-ery	aw-ful
harm-ful	essent-ial	mart-ial	elig-ible	flex-ible
bas-ic	domest-ic	clar-ify	class-ify	caps-ize

Suffix Bingo

civil-ize	form-less	friend-less	argu-ment	develop-ment
foolish-ness	happi-ness	disastr-ous	fam-ous	clerk-ship
friend-ship	awe-some	★	burden-some	celebra-tion
informa-tion	lov-able	prob-able	extens-ive	select-ive
diction-ary	vocabul-ary	loc-ate	oper-ate	magni-fy

Suffix Bingo

critic-ize	organ-ize	grace-less	sleeve-less	encamp-ment
entertain-ment	kind-ness	neat-ness	joy-ous	nerv-ous
horse-man-ship	relation-ship	★	four-some	hand-some
na-tion	rela-tion	regrett-able	extens-ive	vocabul-ary
rel-ate	surg-ery	sin-ful	spec-ial	vis-ible